List & Story

For information about permission to reproduce selections from this book,
contact *permissions* :

Stephen F. Austin State University Press
P.O. Box 13007, SFA Station
Nacogdoches, TX 75962
sfapress@sfasu.edu
www.sfasu.edu/sfapress
936-468-1078

Project Manager: Kimberly Verhines
Cover Art: *Written Word*, Karen Kunc

ISBN: 978-1-62288-307-3

First Edition

List & Story

poems

HILDA RAZ

STEPHEN F. AUSTIN STATE UNIVERSITY PRESS

Here, hands full of sand, letting it sift through
in the wind, I look in and say take this, this is
what I have saved, take this, hurry.

— from "Prayer" by Jorie Graham

We are afloat
On our dreams as on a barge made of ice,
Shot through with questions and fissures of starlight
That keep us awake, thinking about the dreams
As they are happening. Some occurrence. You said it.

— from "My Erotic Double" by John Ashbery

Contents

Three

Four

List & Story

One

Autobiography

I've stolen a chair for you, sawed off the arms.
For breakfast stirred up plovers' eggs. Once
I flew to the moon in order to press your hands to her face.

I strung a magic key around my neck for my roller skates.
On my feet they clanked and threw sparks on the sidewalk.
My mom wore an apron when she wasn't wearing gloves.
I wore silk to the dance midnight blue with a keyhole neckline, a soft bow.

I married for the childbed and didn't die.
I walked out the door on my own two feet.

Alaska wove color through the sky.
The dog sled team at a full run shat frozen turds that missed me.

Up again at night I learned hot milk beats tea every time.
The walls all color wore well and framed up paintings I accumulate.

My house has a bedroom.
Much of my life is over.
Pleasing others is my greatest sin.
When my ribs knit I swore never again to surrender. I lied.

My knee healed with a scar.
Four husbands vanished on horseback but the crops didn't fail.
Winter is a season like any other.
Now spring is all. Spring moving into summer.
Sleep in wind in voices.

What's under pressure breaks out in cactus flowers.
Ants abound in the arroyos and coyotes.
Some of what I couldn't stand to lose I lost.
In every room a pencil.

The Spa of the Three Widows

1.   The Spa of the Three Widows

At lunch this year as anyone can see
or I do draped in a black shawl
that these friends have lost on the grief diet
the weight of one healthy adult man
the one missing from each of their sides
of the patio table where we're sitting.

They bend together over their burgers
— chopped beef or vegetable — and salad
no wine this time   to discuss the past year
when their husbands have taken by the hand
Death and been dispatched by his tools:
disease for one, collapse for another,
and for the third a fall from a cliff.

Behind my shawl I speculate
about the sulfur tubs in the meadow
beyond the patio where we dine
a specific said the brochure for a bad back.
Too much to carry I think listening to the widows.

2.   The Widows Call Me Butch

They have deposited the insurance checks, signed the forms,
spent tens of thousands to settle the estate, pay hospice,
hospital, doctors' bills, equipment rental fees, the nurses.
Their lawyers are cleaning up. His children have split the spoils.
Soon they will carpet the den, move his desk to the basement.
Their brooms have swept salt from the floors of their bedrooms.

Now it's time for them to work on me, still innocent. By butch
they mean *not feminine* — my posture, clothes, my presentation.
They can help me look better even at my age. They hold up
turquoise T-shirts and pale pinks to check for color
a bronze lipstick and nail polish. At their direction
I buy everything and add a sea-foam fleece jacket
cut close to my curves, warm and inexpensive.
Each night my red phone hums as I call my husband.

3.   The Widows Shop for Makeup at Sephora

They wear shorts and sweatshirts with the name of our beach
embroidered on their pockets   two navy, one sea-blue.
They turn up their shiny faces to the salesgirls
for the application of color to their eyelids.

They are absolutely still
seated on cretonne stools so the scarlet,
zinced purples, buff and tan can be applied close to their lashes.
Their eyes are transformed, all green and blue iris, as they open
to the fluorescent light. They buy brushes thin as a fingernail
in a kit for travel and blush compacts set with gold filigree.
Then they blot the sore places under their eyes with Kleenex.

4.   A Widow Weeps

Ophelia wears Mephisto sandals that rub her foot sore over a vein
a big pain that seems to erode her calm.
Later in the car while the others go into the drugstore for bandages to cover
I loosen the strap on her shoe by a notch.

From the backseat she says, Don't speak!
Then wails. I am stone silent as instructed.
But when her small hand pushes between the seats

I take it and hold on. Her pain shudders between us.
What will I do? I say all the fragments of the prayers
I know to beg for the edges to dull.

Artemisia returns with a bag.
Clio unpeels the tape   positions the gauze and presses.
Silence. Then we go on to the beach.

5.   The Widows Dance

The waves have been flat all afternoon
the sky a dulled mirror. We have lain
in the light for hours protected by hats

and towels and shirts. We have slept
and talked and now we are walking
and looking down to find stones in the shapes
of hearts, or those wishing stones with halos
stretched front to back or up and down
or the flat ones for skipping on water.
I pick up the ones most resembling fudge
with stripes of coconut that we buy in the shops
sweet to hold under the tongue.

We have walked along the wet sand
until the white cliff in the distance is just above us
and the tide pool has filled with muscle, a swirl
that pulls us back hard. We hold on and push back.

In the distance one widow is dancing. The sun
has come out and makes of this vista a dazzle
but we can see her flirting with the waves.
Maybe he is there under the surface.
Maybe she can see him. Or maybe she is alone.
We reach to hold hands and run to join her.

6. For Heaven's Sake

Okay, we're sitting by the window   wind a blow
through our hair   when what should we hear
but the sound of blade-chop through air   go figure
so we decide to swim   but another interruption

children's screams on the grass below   go figure
then we decide on lunch   who has the coupons?
we'll wait   and we find them   but what happened to the key

missing   go figure   did we put down our bundles on the counter
or did we   what did we do last night after gin & tonics?
Imagine our subjects of conversation include sex   and abuse
but never the deaths of husbands or their defections.

7. First Days Back

I come home from the beach
to my spouse who is alive and vigorous.
Thereafter two days of antibiotics.
The spring comes on.

Each day arrives in a shower of pollen.
The birdbath water is covered. The Norfolk pines
put out for the season are packed at the forks with yellow.

Everywhere, birds: robins, cardinals (one flew
at the windshield as I turned into our driveway,
a streak of flame), and here should follow the list. Omissions.

All night thunder, lightning, dreams and hard rain.
My wedding bands look so simple worn down.
Should I put back the bright stone beside them?

My morning horoscope counsels patience.
I'm sitting at the keyboard in my black shawl
a nightdress of cotton and nothing more.   Black
shoes with orthopedic arches.   Three rings.

8.   Another Year

We are here . . . and we were never here.
                    —Ann Patchett, *State of Wonder*

Turquoise beads and a golden chain to celebrate
Another year of grief work, an amulet to hold
In the hand. Water rushes downward
Outside our balcony. Green predominates
On the mountain. Those few dead pines
Stand still in wind roiling the ski runs
Now tucked up in color.

Last night's clap and sear
Left three rides on the mountain
Broken. Such a storm!

Because they don't ask
They buy everything decorative.

Their bodies are thin also
Lines on the face where lines hadn't been.

The one who bends over by the roadside
Wears a size two special order.
The one who drives now
Has her fist closed around the amulet.
The other rests, smiles and sings along
In the back seat of the rental, a Cadillac —

Why not? — as the ocher and cerise and magenta
Shopping bags shift in the trunk's shadow
And they navigate the mountain's curves.

Transportation

My father bought a wagon to deliver
groceries, then the shoe store's leathers,
the mercantile's piles of rugs and towels
or anything else those neighbors needed
carried from one place to another.

Then he got a truck, more trucks, and a terminal building,
a phone and typewriter and billing pads,
and put his mother to work in the front office with
an adding machine, a gas pump and a motto:
"We move everything but the world."

He bought a Packard, broke his back
doing some fool thing in the alley,
married Dolly, pretty but helpless
and over years moved the family from
Harvard Street, behind the skating rink,
to Highland Heights, in spite of covenants
against Negroes, Italians, and Jews.
Nobody ever stopped him.

Somehow money piled up, enough
to keep his widow and child for many years,
until the fleet of trucks and buildings
with his name and motto in rolled gold
stopped, were shuttered, sold.

Where is he now, a sliver of bone
and serge dug into a closed cemetery's dirt?
Or reborn as some ambitious boy
in Agra, with a taxi, ready to transport

tourists and their stuff
wherever they tell him to go
or wherever he wants them to go.
And here's a survivor carrying stories
from one life to another, yours, readers.

Home

Well,
I tried and tried for years
but the wallpaper wouldn't stick
the hanging lights were ugly
kitchen and bathroom tile
turned yellow in light.
That house wouldn't have me.

I opened many windows
moved myself from stale room to room
threw back chintz curtains then sheers
sat in my mother's princess armchair
trailing wisps of Joy perfume
stolen from her dressing table
my thumb in a book. Papa's
leather club chair dragged to a place
on the carpet nobody could see.

They were so glad to see me go.
They bought me a plane ticket
and a trunk they helped
fill with clothes I chose unwisely
and they got me to the airport.
Ten months later
my English teacher
husband unlocked
our apartment door.

Go

The year I was eighteen
twelve months of love
magic in leaves I stretched for
reaching upward
to pause
in early dusk
on Boylston Street
walking to Charlesgate East
the year I turned eighteen
"alive" in Hebrew numerology
as my father died.

How leaves that autumn
brightened their yellows and reds
to color light overhead
each day on my walk home.
I carried the future with me
damp luminous sticky redolent.
Still my father died.

What could I know of solitude
of stillness that season?
The sprint of life.
The pain of arriving.

Late September

At the screen door the fat squirrel watches me.
The year turns day by night by day
cold in the early morning, hot at noon, warmer as night comes on.

We watch the TV screen flicker. Action and reaction. Drama.
Always a corpse. Always the rush of attraction. Always the bumbling detective.
We love each other. One of us moves badly.
Is this is old age? Let us grow older.

Somewhere in the world our genes replicate.
No voices here echo ours.
Ristras fill the autumn markets.
The broiler releases the scent of ripe peppers roasting.
Heavenly this place we've come to this season.
Grouse warble under the brush pile.
Are they paying attention to the hawk?
He pays attention.

You ask for four small pears, ripe.
And tomatoes, heirlooms, their shoulders cracked with burgeoning, ripe, ripe.
Fresh corn, last of the season.
Basil-infused olive oil, baskets of purple garlic heads, wreaths of dried herbs.

Well, another autumn aesthetic.

As a young bride I wandered the markets in a coastal city:
barrels of fish, barrels of mussels. Blood on the pavement
near butchers where I bought some of our provender.
Apples my friend gave away to beggars on the overpass, sometimes a flat of
    strawberries.
Our fingers were sticky from tasting, try this
and this. We tried everything offered.

Photograph

The grassy hill descended from the brick garage
down steps to the back door of the kitchen.
Shrubs bordered the foundation.
The two girls wore jeans over filmy underpants
lace cream satin bras under their T-shirts.
They were going to a wedding, one the bride
the other her attendant. But not just yet.

They walked down arm in arm, one's head
nodding to the other's shoulder, air a pressure
on their limbs. One of them had to marry.

The morning air was chilly, the garbage can
they picked up, one each side, was heavy
in their hands and balance hard to keep
going down, the clanging as they walked.

Here we go alone, and like it better so

This life is said to be
in order to cultivate the desert
educate the inhabitants,
work together by day
and by night to sport.

So the term comes to an end.
The end of the conglomerate
of bodies all with deep pockets
all ready or perhaps
not ready to fill them with
the making up of shapes
and the casting of them down.

The season of drabs begins.
And oh we are grateful
for light when it comes
the slow unfolding of
the elongated sheen
of the amaryllis bud in the window
turning his head so discretely
to Zeus — is that his name?
The one necessary for the inevitable unfolding
in the pocket
the vernix licked off by the rub
on some texture at the bottom of the bombazine;
is that fabric used any more for lining suits
the enfoldings at seams, the outpouching at wrist
or waist?

Nevertheless the sky
is discovered to be different
in the morning or at evening
when walking toward the horizon
at the base of the hill, the bottom
of the street, the verge of the playground,
alone at last, and just now on the curb
the residue of the last car speeding
toward the garage, the snow packed down
by the car and the solitary dog's paws
as he rushes to his bowl by the fire.

Flowers of Immortality, Eau de Parfum by Kilian, $235 for 50ml

Shivers of flank and shoulder
already drawing absence nearer

— Linda Bierds, "Simulacra"

We think they are delicious, these traces of freesia and peach,
evoking an utopia where people like us live apart from the world
of supermarkets and beachballs, waking at dawn
to rediscover the moon gone pale from wandering
sinking now into the mountains by our house.

On the porch is a daybed covered in chintz
where you're welcome to sleep all night
below the blazing spectacle, no gas or electric stink
to disturb stars in their patterns, striding widelegged,
waists belted, or mounted, or rocking away the end
of a journey we've been making so many years in the dark.

Or you may decide to doze away the morning, or
early afternoon, after you've smelled then devoured
a white peach martini, one of a set of three on a fan of flowers,
blossoms on the clay plate left out for you on the railing.

Or late afternoon, your hiking boots unlaced,
poles resting against the rose crystal lampshade
on the wicker table, the left one slowly settling
to the floorboards, the scent of white musk seeping
into your head as you sink ever closer to bouquets,
freesia in jars set by your body, bundles of organic
carrots to feed you in the coming company
of shade and philanthropy, pure loveliness, vanilla traces,
black currant, even the Tonka Bean, a live iris outlined in paint,
yourself gone forever, if ever hospitable,
the angels

Two

Women and Poetry

Among all my desires at the time . . . one of the strongest was to put my
full trust in someone; in some man.

— Sigrid Nunez, *The Friend*

They want to be told what's what by a man,
women at the north end of the table nodding together,
one so newly married she writes as if the poem
is her writing hand, lonely for the ring.

I wanted to be told what's lovely by a man
as I was by my famous teacher who taught women,
especially the beauty seated on his right, to incite riot.
Her pain seemed an Ars Poetica,
her poems all naked body, enticingly sensual,
flushed in sun and shower, come from the pool in stanza one
to become in stanza two an erect and threatening penis
in a changing room shared by a man and a girl.
Was she the child? we wondered. What difference to the poem?

In my class, we sat together in a darkening room, late afternoon.
I am trying to love poetry as a stay against confusion,
flesh for now a stay against death, as lightning, incipient storm
with its causal gods, breaks closer to morning.

And now I write alone in the kitchen with only that growl to push me.
No man's voice here, no transformation, only poetry.

Women's Lib

Women turned their loyalties from their father's clothes, huge discarded shirts
They had been missing.

All night dreaming the map of the future their subject had been the artist at work
In a room under the stable.

It is vital to pull yourself up by your own roots.

We were making love in the weeds, slamming the daisies flat.
Milkweed swollen then bursting. Outside birds.

Mostly the television is on, but we didn't notice.

We went to the movies.
Someone in the back row touched my arm,
"Let them eat cake." And then I got angry.

Feathery trees embroidered on batiste:
Old clothes in a poetic mode passed out of fashion.

Blessed be the womb put to use or not. Now dance.

Collaboration

This one writes, steps up, steps back.
The other holds the pad still, a blank.
The fear of pencils is one's contribution. I can't.
Shut up, says the other curtseying. I can.

They do, these two. Look here's their book.
I can read, says one. I can talk, says the other.
To celebrate, one wraps fingers around a glass.
The other waits for steak.

One pushes the other, picks up a knife, hungry.
The other plays with salad.
One holds an apple very still.
Good job, says the other, fingers the handle.

The apple peel falls into a lovely spiral.
Already the other is pushing it towards disposal.

Women and the Global Imagination

Her weight compares to no universe.

— Valerie Martínez

I am thinking, looking in the mirror at the women behind me
coming and going, what do they say? What do they wear?
Robes, or I see rolled-up khaki shorts at the south end of the room.
Do we speak a common language?

"I tattooed my eyelashes on, I'm older and my eyes stream with allergies."
Another woman reaches out her hand to me, to interlace fingers.
She took the drivers' test at 35, passed at 40 after someone fired the driver.
Another woman never took a test, borrowed the truck.

"My daughter's engagement gift was a high-end cell phone.
She had a diamond, one carat plus some points."
And insurance.
And she got an MD degree. Or law.

We took out the garbage. Lived with our aunties.
We farmed, gardened, strapped on infants, plastic water jugs. Pumped.
Got a loom, or better, a sewing machine.
Hemmed tarps and bedding like grandmother did. All Local Products.
The summer was scorching. The winter froze.
He entered me on the fourth day. Why did he wait?

Computer programming is one way to succeed. Computer parts another.
Weave for the tourist markets.
Fewer couples marry, procreate.
The news is told on TV by a blonde woman in a sweater set.
She wears pearls on Mondays, carries a pink .22 in her pack.
Jets crash, someone kicks an eight-year-old to death, another drives four
        children into the sea.

Really, we're screaming.
Drought again after hail the size of baseballs.
Lean in. Yup, me and my sister, the girls, always the source of trouble.
Relocate us. We'll boil water on the grates we find under houses.

Houses. Mine is different from yours. You don't have one.
Borderlands and coyotes.
"Once our stories were round / but the wolves made them square as
          houses," wrote Diane Glancy.
Let's go, get out. Yurts. The grass is always greener on the other side,
          unless it's sand.
Vitamins and coconut water.

Six decades later, see what we've got. Me, too. Borders.
Let's collaborate against powder.
Mascara. Tattoos. The medical establishment. Drugs. Additives.
          Allergies and opioids.

All messages
as we march
fight for relief.

The Burnt Journals

Each thing has come back to answer for itself.

— Hélène Cixous, translated by Beverley Bie Brahic,
The Day I Wasn't There

Here, the burnt journals.

"She made, at her father's house,
a bird, red felt body, pipe cleaner legs,
green petal feet, and underneath, freestanding,
a tiny piebald baby in a nest."
This bird, without its baby, stands on a shelf
in a cold room next to the remains.

"He stormed around breaking glasses;
the children dropped glue on the table.
My lover arrived late for dinner.
My son followed after him, small shadow."

. . . an ornament, "fifty hours of frustrating work,"
in the shape of a guitar. He hung it on the tree.
The real guitar is hidden in the closet for the child to find
among his overcoats, so he won't forget the maker (he never forgets).

"The great houses lit from within,
all the elaborate paraphernalia (a bride's goods) of life . . .
today, gifts set in high relief against peace —
all gifts, treasure raised from salt, debris.

"I lean on rituals of the house.
Is it possible to live forever in silence — children
drawing new fish in the aquarium and singing, waiting to go out?

"I want to know how women sound inside their heads,
not what they speak to themselves in silence, but what they could say aloud."

An account of two weeks with a lover.
In black crayon, top right, his handwriting.

"One more hour . . . twenty minutes, no more time. I am here."
He waits for me, dressed to kill. Guns in the house.
He will negotiate the contract. He will sign much paper.

Night dream: she has given birth, is nursing. Many details.

"She sits in the rocking chair.   From the shut closet, a cry.
In the closet, wrapped in a snowsuit, under the zipper, one of the twins
she gave birth to, this child in her arms. One twin died, she remembers,
but this one is alive and mewing, a swollen belly, a perfect little head, a face.
She'd forgotten him.

"No. I can fix everything. She can nurse this one, too.
The rest of the dream is his little face turning away.
We must tell someone, take him to hospital, tubes into his belly, he can be saved."

Awake now. The sun is loud. Morning.

April, decades later. He burned the journals. I am long gone.

"That human phrases or even a word carry doses of malevolence is well established . . .
The poison circulates via points of resemblance or coincidence between all animated
beings and more particularly by the word I which is in every mouth."
— Hélène Cixous

Dear Sky

I'm here to say I'm sorry,
A little tune from off Broadway
And 142nd Street where
We walked together to the subway
Years ago. I thought we could
Hold hands. Then you were gone.

Most of the time we lived
Together in the backyard.
Once we made love
Under the lilacs behind the house.

Afterwards I drove around a lot
From here to there, worked hard
To avoid looking up. All night
Every night you were gone.   No surprise.
In the middle dark I'd sneak to the garage
Release the hand brake on the Buick
Roll down the driveway to the street.
Who could see? Who'd care?
You were there across town I knew it
Somewhere behind clouds
Your eyes like lights.
I'd drive to the park, look up.
How much I miss you.

Now that I've moved away you're still with me.
I'm not afraid anymore.
How heavy you were on my body.
How burnt I was from exposure.

April

Pale blooms on trees poets sheltered among
to become floral on their book jackets. We girls too
stooped among lilacs for the camera, to show we were Nature.

Photos of cousins among peach blossoms in the backyard
were caught in a silver frame. Next, here we are too,
posed among branches of magnolia, a nest.

Did we forgive ourselves later, our skirts filled with scent
as we crouched over the incense burner to get ready?
Flower cups blooming on cactus as red as we were at center.

I never said I'd live among blooms for long, did I?
In *Blade Runner* he said, "Time to die" as he did,
that beautiful automaton.

One Toe, Crooked

Let me tell you how it is with me:
a bad back, spine like a snakeskin
shed in the shadow of a pinelet,
weakened innards, a liver fit for soup,
and a brain the size of a lentil. The worst
is the one toe, crooked like a staff
carried too long by shepherds.

One day, a fine mid-autumn
with sun's eye full open against air's chill,
I took to the woods to find my dinner.
What with one thing and another
I swayed and shimmered my way along
the path, gravel stuck to my knees from a fall,
my Felt shoes catching stones.
But still, I got to the gate where geese cross
coming home from the pond.

What would do me that night?
I was one only, with an oven fit
for a child with money, my prize.
Each night I lit it with a fagot
of willow and some wormwood leaves.
It had an iron basket suspended over the fire,
good for roasting corn and potatoes.
Tonight I was hungry against the chill coming.
No ice yet, that was full winter
but now a clutch of eggs to boil in the kettle?

Truly then I saw a girl
lovely as a stalk of silver grain
come around a corner that an oak made

with my barn wall. She carried a bundle
squirming like a peck of tadpoles,
and clutched to her chest a stack of books
bound with a strap. She saw me
as a wraith and ran. Was I a wraith?
My toe hurt like hell itself gaped open.
But Ectoplasm I wasn't. Plain flesh.
Still, she was afraid. Then I could see her babe's
mouth open, its cries louder with each bounce,
the flannel it was bound with coming loose.

As I watched, standing bent over my toe,
she dropped the books. The belt around them opened.
Pages fanned out on the ground
like parchment put to flame.

What did all this mean in the daylight?
The girl, her babe, the lost books cascading
and over everything pain ascending,
covering our light, all that hope,
the future somehow gone dark as a cavern.

I bent over the mess, began to gather it up.

List and Story

1.

First we must go for flowers
To the nursery. Spring is here.
My heart speaks, an utterance
Packed with many meanings,
As the begonias have petals
Some one color, some another
And all blending into that plant
You choose for the hanging basket.

My brother at fifteen went to war.
He was an infantryman, a photographer.
He opened the camps with his fellows.
Then he came home. He lived at home.
He lived in his bedroom. He studied.
He graduated. He married and . . .
You know that story. Sons.
At forty he took up a gun
Into his mouth and pulled the trigger.
He was in the woods where the bears go.
He drove the old car. He didn't leave a note.
He was gainfully employed. His sons . . .
That utterance. And then peace.

The red petals have fallen. The flushed
Petals remain. Leaves like steak knives,
Serrated, fleshy, the darkest green.
We go to the garden with our children.
We have graduated. We have married.
The garden is our pleasure and utterance.
Marriage, that pleasure. The making of food,

The making of the yolk and white of one egg.
The whirling of the mobile under which we
Make our children. Such pleasure moves.

Let us tear the garden into ribbons.
Let us transplant the white daffodils
With their bonnets that bend backward.
Let us move the magnolia corms.
Let us divide the bulbs and the peonies.
Who will take the children. I will, I will.

2.

Who let the monster into the house?
Who cooks the food for him, shops,
Plays the flute, drives the tumbrels?
Who folds into the hay blankets, drinks
The red wine, wears the jewels? Who
Hangs the blade over the fireplace
With its jeweled hilt, braided scabbard?
Who watches the savaging of the children?
Utterance. One child. Where were you
To say no, leave a note, take up the gun?

The body of the flowers in the hanging basket
Is multiple, blue stars and anise, pansies
And feverfew, the hanging vines of sweet potato.
Its utterance is heavy moving in wind, creaks.
The children play in the garden, on the swings,
In the sandbox. One carries a greasy bag in his fist,
Bologna and chips, a slippery bottle of pop.
They lock the door. They cavort on the rug.
And it was evening. The monster reigns.

Utterance: spring. Summer, fall. Winter
Silence and the smell of balsam. Pastries
That you roll out on the floor, shape into log,
Apply frosting, display. Bow. Décolletage.
And it was morning. The children under the tree.
Gifts and more gifts. The timbrels and bells.
Bach and the great Germans. Some candles.
Some fire. Who let the monster into the house
With his axe, his dragged tree, sticky sap?

    3.

I slid down the shut door, locked it.
I hit the floor, stopped. I wept.
She thanked me, that child with blood
On her cheek. She thanked me with her bruised tongue.
She thanked me with her utterance and disappeared.
Never again. Never again. Never again. And so forth.

And it was morning and it was evening of the fourth day.
The basket was hanging on the porch in the heat of the day.
In the night, in the cool garage with its lowered door,
A moat between night and the house, lurking . . .
That utterance. A gun, that utterance. Disbelief,

That utterance. And in the house the children . . .

And now the story is over. Silence. Penance.
Utterance, the page and the oranges. Pears and wafers.
Forty years in the desert of the sandbox where cats dig.

Six Objects in a Gold Foil Box

— Barton James Raz, 1927–1966

1.

"That amethyst geode is like a drugstore urinal."
Does she mean Duchamp?

To me, the skin is spotted like an outlandish zebra.
(Spots on a hide ought to be striped white and black.
An inert zebra is too heavy to turn over. I might be mistaken.)
The heart is purple when we pry it apart.

2.

His mother's best brooch this one isn't.
But we all like it whorled on the bosom of her house dress.
All pattern, swirls of cream and brown where her breast
— is that the right word? — would jiggle but doesn't.
What is it catches light from the window?

3.

Pumice? The caldera of a volcano?
What ought to be good feels bad, all scratchy.
The pillow is supposed to fit spots behind knees, on rough elbows.
Scrubbed hard red stripes interrupt skin.

The cat spends hours reaching into the plant pots for something
worm-eaten, dropped from the pin oak in autumn before the pots
      come back in.
So heavy the pots, so light the acorns she tosses up onto the tile floor
where they skitter. In summer, when pots go back out, what's left will
      begin to sprout.

4.

A faint chime, ruffled by fingers stirring scarves in the drawer.
Look. Among the silk welter:
a tiny top hat, a filigree bridge, a sailboat with a moving jib,
a bust of Lincoln fingernail size, and a lamb.
Scooped out of the silk, circling your wrist,
a jingle as she fusses with your hair.

5.

Oh, empty bowl on the piano shawl,
etched crystal chrysanthemum,
the cold blue multiplies diamonds on plush curtains,
a plum scrim between what's present what's merely absent this season.

In a square state, let's say Highball,
folks come down to the river to drink.
They bring cups to ring on stones on the bank.
Something crashes. Something wearing purple falls in.
She used to be pretty. Now she is a zebra
with spots, nothing human at all.

Mirror hung sideways, how does your light quicken?
Your prisms absorb all heat in the room!
So pretty the glow we can't see by.
Whose idea, big boy? Not mine.
I admire you from below, listen for your shatter
as the silk cord lets go.

6.

Can Eeyore be a cheetah, please? I ask Nurse,
but she doesn't answer. The answer is no,
no matter how much I want it.
My jaws are firecrackers in a wooden crate stamped 1,000 LBS. on the lid.
If we wait long enough, I whisper under the coverlet. If only I can grow up.

7.

Put everything back in the box right now, under the foil lid.
I'm Pandora, ready to slam down the top.
Inside are virtues and vices, who cares which?

I do, says the tin soldier with the red plush heart.
I'm not a pin cushion. I'm a defender.
Help me up! Let me out, Queen Bee!

The zebra with spots has a jeweled heart, all glitter and roil.
The brooch, neon headlights for eyes,
blinks on the highway verge,
all loopy possibilities,
all mammal, all explorer, all body.

Wait! I'll be his brain I promise him,
my pen writing a house for him.
He's all gone.
But I'm conjuring broad fields from the charm bracelet, loofa, mirror,
the rotten acorns, the empty bowl, the glittery brooch, the geode, his
        flensed skin.
I promised him. I promise him.

War

Graceful but badly armed
soldiers hit the field
to be slaughtered of course
like vets who die later
guns in their mouths.

Beloveds have been made ash.
Family settles down
to the facts of property.
Drapes blow at windows.
Probity.
Winter driveways
shoveled by hired men.
And the shelves papered
with oilcloth flowers.
Sickened by meats
some have new clothes
to cover their bones.

News is stories
of victims and survivors
faces we know.
Caps on their heads.

Let us take up the veil.
Wail to waste hours.
Breath is soul some say
so if body falls soul falls.

Who wants the wars we make?
Who wants not to leave the field?
Who wants to live with heroes?

I want to live in fields with beetles
who scurry under counters
oblivious that their lives are saved
by sending away the exterminator.
What good is care for the world?

A Covey of Scaled Quail

The bedroom shade is half drawn.
Snow interrupts the field
Cliffs of sand held together
Intermittent shrub and rock.

We wait by the window
Frame of a white falling
A rush of cold against which
Our breath moves.

Now dark interrupts the snow.

Under the juniper slowly
The odd bird scurrying
Then two, then a group
That vacates in ranks the dark under
And goes into fog. Covey. Many.

Where has this covey come from?

Dry air sucks up snow then leaves
What falls to stay a while as we do
Inhabitants of another intermittence.
Footprints to discover at dawn
As cold drops over the mountain
And we wake to watch another day.

Another Story

First he was coming out the door.
Then he was on the path, his hand outstretched.
Smiling.

High summer.
Then six months, start to finish.

Now she identifies him prior to burning.
Then she goes home to flowers, the funeral meats.
Imagine the sight of the city beyond the windows.
Imagine his harpsichord in the music room.
Their several flutes on the shelf.
Imagine the sunset in those windows.
Day two, day three, day four.

The widow slept with their daughter two nights, holding hands.
Death seemed to burn away her life.

But she would revive, like a foot asleep under the weight of a body.

Three

The Impossibility of Stasis

1. Stone under the tongue.

2. A scarf of sparks to set the house afire.

3. Breath exhaled then held and held.

4. Breath inhaled, a gasp, paroxysm.

5. The infant crowns, a last spasm.

6. Peppermint dissolving.

7. Spray, the apex of a wave.

8. Notes in the air of a chilly hall.

9. Body suspended en pointe.

10. Thuds onto the floor of the stage.

Now moving toward the audience, flying.

The Past and the Future

Once I wore a dress of iridescent icy peau de soie;
The sleeves were shirred, short on my dark arms.
After a season, salt rotted the silk into pure blue.

Yesterday on Skype I talked to you for an hour.
You looked like a Whitman sampler lid,
All color-blocks, modern art and candy,
A grid. You stayed together through shifts of pixels,
You abroad, me at home.

Last night, great flashes and percussion in our sky.

If I should lose the accompaniment, I would stop.
No rest but cymbals then silence.

Watching Bulls / Falling in Love with the Dead

"Stormy Wing sure can ride!" shouts the TV.
Beethoven is playing in the next room so the bulls
seem almost tender as they put their feet down hard
either side the head of this cowboy they've just bucked off.

Outside finches on the feeder chirp in the shadow
of a Cooper's Hawk over quail chicks' chirr and chuckle
as their papa shakes his topknot, fusses to call them under the brush.

Oh but now I remember them all, a parade of lovers shaking their butts,
lifting hats at the last minute! Sweet ones.
I sit still to remember my part in this bucking and charging:
What a ruckus at the best tables, me dressed in silver peau de soie,
feather buckles on velvet shoes tapping the hems
of tablecloths falling onto the plush carpets.
Or running alleys at midnight, chasing coins of moonlight,
always restless, wearing out the season's sandals
cinched around my skinny ankles, feet tanned and calloused,
hitting the still hot pavement hard.

On TV, Chicken-on-a-String, the bull with the fawn belly,
twists under the strap Cowboy Bill adjusts so carefully
before the ride, his broken hand taped,
the moistened rope laid carefully between fingers and thumb
before the gates open. "Let's get 'er done," they yell
to each other, switching rides just like the boys did, or I did
once a year or more, sometimes a month or a weekend.

They were easy to forget, that's the truth,
riders dead to me as I ran on through pasture gates,
bulls distant on the horizon, cowboys sitting on fences.

Uh oh. One falls off, rolls under the gate, and out.
Clowns divert the bull. It was close to the end he tucked his palm under,
smiled and spun from the core what looked like a flexible, perfect ride.
But that centrifugal force pulls you to the side every time
and

      almost

           always

                off.

A Conversation about Text

To start a harvest my mind is clearer now on how to proceed. I look forward to the second half of what might be a year's project.

— Michael James

Or a life's. To finish a project
suggests the rest of breath.

To envision this story properly
you need at least three veils
draped over holes of rust.
To open up a doorway
first wood then a splintering.
Through the opening
at the point of what now we'll call a window
we see a garden or a painting of a garden
— ekphrastic this text —
through which the miniature magnolia called stellata
opens its stars to be stilled
spilling light.

"I am energized about this project
more so tonight than at any time before.
My mind is clearer now on how to proceed.
Time has become a big issue with me
as each day passes. I don't think
I don't think I've ever felt it
so strongly as I do now
since adopting this new life."

Time is stilled.
The background figure through the window
has turned her back on the foreground
where a huge man squats

his weight entirely static.
He's a balance for her absence
though he thinks her nape is exquisite
individual hairs ascending into a mass of dark silk.

Imagine our surprise for then we hear the rusty hinge or maybe two
on this side of the opening to the garden
or the picture of the garden on which might be hung
we can't know exactly how
the veils.

"And I wonder too if it isn't just age
and the increasing sense there's less time left
each second must be maximized.

"But then the impulse just to find a hidden place
and camp out for days or weeks — what a dream!"

The woman stirs
the silken hairs at the nape of her neck stir.
(How can they be seen moving through the veils?)
They do and the bark of the dogs in the garden
is barely heard by the figures on the porch
farther back at the glass tables eating lunch
fresh greens and a quiche
drinking water
nodding toward the water below
barely seen in the distance but seen. The talk.

"So I mention this in appreciation of YOUR time,
which to you is no doubt worth its weight in gold,
as it is to me. I am energized about this project
more so tonight than at any time previous.
And I resent that duties call me away from my studio
just when I feel I could pull something forward.
Well, I'll work on it nevertheless, in absentia."

The man in the picture is rising is moving to the window
behind the woman or the picture of the garden or
toward what we now see is a fireplace mantel
over which is hanging something metal gilt.
His bulk moves past the back of the woman's head.
Then his arms rise to unfasten a sheen.

I ask you is this horizontal balance
a necessary counterweight of rust
to the presence of the vertical veils
through which we see his fingers
individual then all ten working together
detach gold from the dim hooks and take up the sword?

"Emma," fabric, wool and lace, 1970
Soft sculpture by Dorothea Tanning

What would Molly Bloom think of Emma Bovary?
— Dorothea Tanning

1.

After the huge Oldenburg oilcloth light switch
that sags on the wall of the museum
we turn the corner to find "Emma,"
tiny pink cloth belly without a head, in a nest of lace.
The belly button is stitched in. Here's the signage etched on a plaque:

". . . the semi-abstract sculpture with its rounded breast, abdomen with navel and limb-like extrusion suggests a disassembled and reconfigured female form. Femininity is accented by the addition of a lace garment that encircles the form. This bizarre distorted and somewhat monstrous body can only have been born from the realm of the unconscious. Emma [is] 'sur' real – above and outside the real world as we know it."

Where is the breast? I don't see it. Yes, now.
The single bust defined by a row of stitching.
We're in the Nelson-Atkins Art Gallery.
The new Bloch wing is carved from light.

2.

This wing of the museum displays the work of masters
whose breath mingled with our own for a while
in an age we shared: later contemporary art.
A Rothko from his dark period, a year of his life
before his suicide, 1963. And here, around the corner is
this little recumbent cushion on a tall plinth called "Emma."

I think it's a memento of months carrying a child, pregnant,
the headless whole no larger than a pin cushion

someone brought as a gift after the birth. A tomato or a strawberry.
I had become fruit, vegetative, immanent for months
and now delivered of a masterpiece. No lace.
Dorothea Tanning found the lace quite useful as a nest.
I have been a nest.

3.
In the shops:

to celebrate long life, a birthday,
a green white and red quilt made in the nineteenth century
in a pattern called "Gizzards and Hearts"

is charming, two faint and large rusty stains
at either end to celebrate the life of the body,
mind busy reclaiming and naming mementoes.

4.
The fires rage in the hills above Santa Barbara
where a room is reserved, a flight booked
through flaming air — all to cancel, of course.
The hotel clerk says he is leaving to join the firemen.
The hotel is filled with evacuees.

I will not be an evacuee.

5.
I will not be an evacuee, not yet.
Did Dorothea Tanning think of Emma as evacuated?
Is her lace pubic hair part of a lace cushion? Emma is tiny
in the company of huge paintings, gigantic sculpture.
She is displayed on a plinth. She is surreal. An abortion?
Surely not. The birth of the self?

6.
She was 101 when she died, her maker,
Dorothea Tanning. Her website flashes
pictures of her work. Two books
of poems published in her lifetime,
which also is mine. She stayed alive
until the last minute. As she died
I gazed at "Emma," said yes out loud.

Four

Nick Spencer, Two Days Dead

"He took himself," Richard says
at dinner — a shrimp boil, andouille sausage,
steamed corn and new potatoes, high summer.

Moon flowers stud the bushes each side of the front door,
moist blossoms seeming too heavy to open.

To the left, on entering, and above your head,
tiny white flowers — are they moon flowers, too,
a variant, full-open? So when Richard says later,
over pear ices, "next life is different," he means
next human life, doesn't he?

In the backyard, from the dining-room window,
bittersweet climbs both male and female,
established enough to go on bearing, as Richard says,
through generations of us.

On the table, platters of clay hold shrimp
in mounds, pink, & golden corn cobs broken into servings,
and pale browns, the potatoes, like nipples.

So many subjectivities, shifting portals
made of layers, like silk, and Nick caught and broken
through to the next layer — like petals like berries.

And we here together talking, swaying forward
to try to bring ourselves home.

The da Vinci Moon

The da Vinci moon is rising by Saturn, its pierced mate.
They are lovely, a slipper moon as mother would say
thin as the edge of a Mercury dime.

Tonight she is smiling her sliver or slipper at the bottom of her face.

Beloved paces in and out of rooms looking from the windows
at the sky west where the sun is making a rosy stripe at the horizon
then east at our lady moon smiling over the arroyo.

Soon when dark comes, rooms with their furniture will disappear.
Out the windows the perimeter of the moon shows a chipped halo
or something else I can't say.

A Meditation on Respect

Whatever else you think, think this: death comes soon.
There. I've said it.
                            And on this morning, sun spilt
gold on grey pebbles under our back window.
Yesterday three Bobcats, mama and two kits,
came there and slept the morning away. I swear!
They came panting with matted fur, skinny, fell
in the shadow our house made, a shade not
much wider than they were, stretched toe to tail.

There. I've finished the first stanza, Rispello.
Eight line blocks, each one eleven syllables.
Some hours later the Bobcats woke, went off,
their backs turned to us watching from the porch,
kits no longer skinny but still small, wind-fluffed
by breath come up to move clouds along the sky.
Below, we tiptoed fast around corners looking
to find them up on the hill. But no, they'd gone.

Here's one example of someone alive, afraid,
counting life up against death with her fingers.
Hear me: that's Bobcats where we live.   Coyotes
we track by listening, rarely see. And crows
as big as hawks. And hawks and eagles. Rabbits.
More. Jackrabbits, twice as big as dogs. And birds.
I could make a catalogue, hummers we feed
with sweets, bright finches, yet why bother? *Death's face*

obscures. Yet now chamisa is in bloom
all over the arroyo. See what I mean? Yellow.
The world is fractals, numbers. Still the world rots.
But is not lost. Enough. Look out. Where cats were,

now on the wall a lizard waits in sun for lunch.
My love is melting sugar in red water
for migrating hummingbirds. Pet in atrium,
sleeping in sunshine, calico coat aflame.

Remember Joseph wore one, a gift, in fear
of his brothers? He was right. Death's robe, no color,
covered him then he was gone — to Egypt, lost.
His jealous brothers and their father also grieved.
A gift of death turned into exile is good?
Do I think I've made an argument for life?
Not here. Not now. Though we are old, many others
die as babes in arms, in gowns, or rags, wrapped close.

Just as Bobcats, so cared for by each other
sleep wove them into one body. Then they go.
As I will, that's the truth, the rub, the whitewash
no one buys. (They favor light enamel crème
that covers better.)
               Reader, will you sing out
a theme from Bach to comfort us listeners
sore from hospital, sickness, stitches, bloody
wounds, recovery sure or not? Bless us.

Meditation

I can't I can't I can't I can't I can't
Who's talking? Shut up, compassion.

Put on socks and shoes meditation

Walking meditation
        Once around the desert
        no dog, nobody

Counting heart stones meditation
        in the basket, on the ground

Walking the dog meditation
        out loud, out loud: listen dog. Metta

May i/she be safe may she/i be happy may she be/feel well may she
        live/die lightly

Gratitude meditation: each day a white stone
        picked up by the front door   by the back garden
        put down on the ground   white stones to a make a mouth:

        If my mouth were as wide as the seven seas
        it would not be enough to praise Thee

Be quiet.   Make lunch.   Notice the thumb, the work of the thumb.
        Notice the edge of the   knife blade

Wash the dishes meditation.   Metta

may our friend be safe may she be happy may she be well may she live/
        die lightly

I can't sit still   death death death death. I can't i can't i can't i
        Who?
        May she walk in the shadow of death and fear no evil thy arroyo
                rock and thy cottonwood staff   comfort

Breathe breathe / breathe breathe

Rauch means soul means breath   is breath   is soul
        breathe breathe / breathe
        until the body / stone
        fractures
        to release

The Mandala of Now

I could get in the car, drive the spring streets to the Lux Art Gallery
Buy sculpture made of books sanded into stones by that one artist.
Or go to the popcorn and ice cream store.

I can sit all afternoon in the long room on a cushion, cat on my lap
To read in the scent of magnolia cut from the lowest branches
Of the old tree by the front door. Or sit and breathe, mind emptied.

How lucky I am in this air-filled body at rest, my mind taking nibbles
As a robin hops down the hill, flies up to the birdbath
Or the thrill of the dove, wide open as she heads for the window
And misses, lifts and flares out.

A Symposium on Love

*"Damn the word," said Justine once, "I would like to spell it backwards as
you say the Elizabethans did God. Call it evol and make it a part of 'evolution'
or 'revolt.'"*

— *Justine*, Lawrence Durrell

Age is an evolution — or devolution — of lust.
To be lost in revolt, as one must be growing up,
invites erotics into the palace of the family.
Air spiked with ecstasy. We all know it.
Then voluble in bed might signify lust
or politics, depending on whether
you live in a hovel where the velocity
of wildlife, certainly a mouse, about its vital business
shadows the movements of governments,

or a hotel, hovering over the chasm
between mountains where we stopped.
Olives. Lupine. The sound of violins
through the balcony window resinous
heard through steam: treatments for the liver.
Into the porches of our ears pours music
reverberating through marble spaces. "That old man
wants to live," whispers a medic
mopping up. His vulpine mask a blur
through silk curtains as he bends over
to lave bodies slippery with oil. He cares for us.

Here in the mountains where we feel free
olives are served in gin straight from the freezer.
The menu reports that olev is an alternative
a citrus fruit found in the garden below.
A solo viola with piano plays at a wedding on the patio.

Is olev a word in another language
an oval fruit used in a harvest ritual
a kind of citron   a renewal   a stand-in for love?

Maybe instead you wrote, "Nearby some wedding party is tuning up.
It's hard to hear their voices. We've enough lunacy on this balcony
overlooking the ceremony to interpret youth and age. Drink up!"
She whispers, "I've loved you for half my life."

To reprise: voluble in bed can signify
the exhaustion of lust and the birth of politics
depending on where you live, a hovel
or next summer's hotel on a coast where olives are eaten
crushed with oil and tomatoes on pasta. Viols can be heard
from a balcony overlooking the river.

In a hotel notebook become a diary you can signify a place
where you stayed one summer, the air an oven
you entered to make love or sleep.
Your bed linens were streaked with damp.
Remember oval windows above his elbow
trimmed with red and yellow light? I don't.

A mirror in the corner showed us at the moment
we became another person tiny and contorted
for a few beats who might change
into an idiot with a harelip or a midget,
a violinist of genius but peculiar, hard to reach
until the world called out to him and he went.
He appears tonight on the program.

Let us return to the moment, please.
Your new partner is to be found at the next table
voluble thank God after months of silence.

What's he onto now? Oh, the volume of trade
on the stock exchange. I'm interested. Are you?

Here in the mountains after sunburnt children with their dogs
are put to bed conversation veers toward the intimate.
Of course the subject is money. A plunging market.
What's to be done? Be patient. The people will speak.
Vox Popular in November. The new red may be black.
Be patient. "I grew up in a Victorian melodrama," overheard
might seem to change the stakes. For me, at least.

In a corner of the room under satin swags that frame the mountains
three women lean toward the axis of their table and whisper.
You can hear their hisses over the swipe of VISA through the bar machine.
If you . . . you'll disappear . . . Escape?
But how? Where do they think they'll go?

Meanwhile the elderly are falling in love.
You can. Erotic is the reverse of deathly.
Dour Mr. Thanatos rents out accordions
at base camp if you've a mind to dance.

And while we're speculating here,
if you have a comrade with a mind so rigid
you can hear the crack on the page as you read
his work, what can you do at 8,000 feet?

Maybe you can write some evolved and looser squiggles
to depict the guy on the plane en route in the next seat
depressed because no one will talk to him
so his head droops onto his chest
seemingly ready to be released into a basket.
Wasn't that the French Revolution?
That guy only wanted to convert us not seduce.

Nearby some wedding party is tuning up.
It's hard to hear over his voice what they're saying.
Certainly we've enough lunacy on this balcony
overlooking the pool. Drink up!
A bridesmaid hands over a hanky. The best man is her.
Their fathers link arms. Their mothers smile.
By now we're sobbing into tissues and taking pictures.

Surely next comes midlife revolt. What do you think?
Oh look.   A moose lopes over the top of the mountain.
The bell for dinner sounds. I've a mind to bolt
this place. Echoes reverberate on the balconies.

You know, I've loved him for half my life.
At the end, it seems the rest of the relatives died.

Pristine

I am sick with worry when you call.
You tell me a story about ears
How the doctor asked about your earaches
Peered in and pronounced "Pristine.
Clean as a whistle." And you were cured.

Because I am a maker of poems
And you are a maker of music
You tell me the word pristine was perfect.
It was the cure.

Yesterday I went to the hospital
To hear my heart beat in her various chambers.
I knew the sounds:
The *Fly Bird* from the right ventricle
The *Go Go* from the left
The *Here I am* from under the rib.

The Sisters

Once there were twelve sisters who lived together.
They were old now, within a decade of beyond old,
but still they were alive.

They slept in a room they'd shared as children.
Each had a life remembered: a beloved, pets,
their own children who were cousins,
who'd summered together at the beach each year
with their papas, their mamas, their aunts.

Now the sisters were old. In the mornings, they'd arise, put on cotton robes,
pull cushions from under their beds to sit on.
Each faced a window.
Each had a bureau just big enough to hold treasures.
Every morning they sat.

One morning the sisters awoke with sore feet. "Ouch," each complained.
Nothing to be done. They looked for their shoes, found tatters.
All day they went barefoot in the garden, in the kitchen, under stars.
When they sat down on their beds before sleep, tired, each found new shoes
sparkled with sequins, sewn Felt. Treasures. Each sister lay down and slept.

Next morning they awoke again with sore feet, their sparkly slippers again tatters.
All day again they went barefoot in the garden, in the kitchen, under stars.
Then, time for bed. Surprise, each found sparkly slippers made of Felt,
some green, some gold, some purple or opal, and many other colors.
They smiled at each other, lay down and slept.

Years passed. The old sisters grew older, their feet knurled and blistered,
piles of old shoes thrown out their windows into the backyard loam,
like mementoes of lives extinguished. Dogs came to sniff and dig.
One dog, a noble beast, carried around a string of tatters in his mouth.

He seemed to dig when nobody watched him. Most of the time
he was invisible. The sisters slept more and more, in light as well as darkness.
In the air, a swirl of soft bells, the sounds of trumpet, rubab and drum.

One midnight, the eldest sister opened her eyes. Surprise. Around her
a whirl of sisters. And the noble dog followed along behind
dragging his tatters. Each sister had a partner, a clattering bone bag,
slender of wrist and ankle, waist and neck, who held her at wrist and waist.
They swung as the dog leapt and wove himself into lacy ropes and shadows.
Were you there? I was. I saw the sisters dance, the dog jump, the bones
        begin to flower.

Talking to each other

Whatever you say next
is an achoo, or an echo
of a voice you've not heard
in a decade, someone gone

or lost or dead, ho, ho, no
matter, the sound is welcome
so long absent and whether
it's saying something in human

speech or not, maybe the chirps
of lazy birds settling down,
you haven't heard anything
like it since you were a body

sloughed off, every cell replaced,
so long soi soi soi shhh air
in your ear or at your temple
so long so long
so long
ago.

First Light

Must we give up desire, ambition, goals,
the invulnerable body, the lack of pain —
pray for it, pray for it — in order to empty mind

learn control of breath, blood, life
continues through plants and beasts, snow
melts, sun rises and sets day in, day out, birds
wing against sun, the sway of the feeders cold
                                        the single sun drop

caught at the corner of the feeders, pink
snared by mountains at sunset
go sit just where I can see pink highlight
coming the crags of dark
oh coming?

Seasons

Spring then winter then spring
all month. We plant flower pots.
We scrape sand from the floor of the garage.
We eat less then more then less again.
Each day birds hit the sun singing.
Rabbits leap around arroyo corners.
Rocks shrink in big winds, big rains.
Is that snow on the mountain?
All the while boundaries lower. Dharma.
The new cat settles in. We merge.

New women, pregnant, are out walking.
Old women suffer for their friends.
Children grow and leave, spring in their blood.
I bow to the light within you.
I bow to the light within you.

Letters from a Lost Language

An alphabet's molecules / tasting of honey, iron, and salt, / cannot be counted—
> — Jane Hirshfield

"Our life in minerals," wrote the poet
to call up the patient sea.
He stands on sand called shore. Salt mustache.
The letters come, are caught, arranged, erase.

Here then is my life in letters. A great weight.
A metal alphabet meaning nothing one can decipher.
(Patience, calls out the poet from the margins.)
One letter like a chair flexes toes. One is a psi.

I have tried all my life
to carry weight from the margins to the center
one letter then another until the click
of the box says stop.

See the hasp of the lock on the transparent door?
See the shadows? Is one a belt buckle?
A woman swimming? One arm
of a scissors. A chair. A man waving.
A clown in a backbend. Dog
behind a bolt.

zzzz says the guard in the box
as he bows his pregnant belly behind Kokopelli
to make an urn.

Shadows move to ease light
from the museum windows.
Soon we will find the metal key.

Again the poet brushes salt into glowing shapes.
Soon the fires will light
and we will return to mineral.

Notes

"The Spa of the Three Widows" is for Pat Emile and Lisa Linsalata.

"Late September" remembers Vera Spohr Cohen.

"Flowers of Immortality" is for Jehanne Dubrow.

In "Women and Poetry," "a stay against confusion" is from Robert Frost.

"The Past and the Future" and "Pristine" are for John Link.

"A Conversation about Text" quotes the quilter Michael James as part of our collaboration, quilt and poem.

"Meditation" is for Lisa Lenard-Cook. The song in stanza eight is a Jewish prayer.

"A Symposium on Love" refers to T. S. Eliot's "in the mountains, there you feel free . . ."

"Letters from a Lost Language" is for Aaron Raz Link and is part of our collaboration based on his assemblage of found forms in cast metal, and label text, arranged on clear shelves in a transparent box.

"The correction of prose, because it has no fixed laws, is endless. A poem comes right with a click like a closing box," W. B. Yeats wrote in a letter.

Thanks to Rodger Kamenetz and Michael Hafftka for *To Die Next to You.*

Acknowledgments

ABQ InPrint, for "Another Story" and "The Sisters"

Askew Poetry Journal, for "Late September"

Numero Cinq, for "A Symposium on Love," Autobiography,"
"Meditation," and "One Toe, Crooked"

Salt, for "A Conversation about Text" (published as "The Bigger Issue
of Time")

Solo Novo, for "A Symposium on Love"

Hyacinth Girl Press, for "Women and Poetry," in *Women Write Resistance:
Poets Resist Gender Violence.* Thanks to the editor, Laura Madeline
Wiseman.

Literary House Press, for "Flowers of Immortality," in *The Book of
Scented Things,* and "Letters from a Lost Language," in *Still Life with Poem.*
Thanks to the editors, Jehanne Dubrow and Lindsay Lusby.

Lost Horse Press, for "Women's Lib," in *Nasty Women Poets: an
Unapologetic Anthology of Subversive Verse.* Thanks to the editors, Grace
Bauer and Julie Kane.

Each book brings its own challenges. This one grew over many miles and
years, from Nebraska to New Mexico.

Thanks to Aaron Raz Link and Lynn C Miller, first and last readers and
collaborators, the former over much of his lifetime, the latter over a
decade.

Thanks to JoAnn Rittenhouse, Ruth Rudner, and Sue Hallgarth for their
writing, reading and friendship. Elise McHugh is a friend to all writers
through the University of New Mexico Press where we have been
colleagues on the Mary Burritt Christiansen poetry series. Lynda Miller,
brilliant artist and editor, enriches my life as she does the lives of all her
friends. Thanks to Kwame Dawes, poet, critic, professor and editor of
PRAIRIE SCHOONER for his ongoing support.

Thanks to John Link, whose music is the ground. Anna Maria Schoenhammer Link and Eva Maria Schoenhammer Link extend the field. Thanks to Maria Schoenhammer for her generosity and to Daire Elliott for his place in my life.

Without friends, silence. Thanks to Carole Simmons Oles, Mary Ellen Capek, Phyllis and Arthur Skoy, Pamela and Kelly Yenser, Pat Emile, Lisa Linsalata, Carol Musrey, Elizabeth Hadas, Em Hall, Helene Stillman and many others whose names are notes through these pages.

Kimberly Verhines as Director of Stephen F. Austin State University Press brought enthusiasm and vigor to the publishing of *List & Story*. Thank you.

Thank you to friend, colleague, and collaborator, the artist Karen Kunc for permission to use her color woodcut, *Written Word*, as the cover of this book.

This book is for Dale Nordyke, companion and ringleader.

CPSIA information can be obtained
at www.ICGtesting.com
Printed in the USA
FSHW012058230320
68405FS